George Clooney

by **Bob McCabe**

CHAMELEON

First published in Great Britain in 1997 by Chameleon Books
an imprint of Andre Deutsch Ltd
106 Great Russell Street
London WC1B 3LJ

Andre Deutsch Ltd is a subsidiary of VCI plc

Printed and bound in Great Britain by
Caledonian International Book Manufacturing Ltd, Glasgow

A catalogue record for this book is available from the British Library
ISBN 0233991727

contents

" Everyone in my family is famous "

George Clooney is a typical example of an overnight success story. Typical in that his overnight success arrived after nearly a dozen years of struggle, disappointment and failure. Fifteen unsold television pilots, recurring roles on seven TV series and a string of movies forever consigned to B movie hell led to him finally donning the cowl of the most financially successful cinema franchise of the past decade, taking over the role of the Caped Crusader in Batman & Robin – via a career-making stint in television's most popular emergency room, of course. It has not been an easy or direct route. But it was a path that he always seemed destined to follow.

'Being famous is no big deal for me,' Clooney told The People. 'Everyone in my family is famous.'

And in their own way, the Irish-American Clooney clan were.

George's father, Nick Clooney, grew up in the golden age of American radio, listening to the popular comics of the day, and longing to be a news broadcaster. His two sisters, Rosemary and Betty, were singers. Their Uncle George was a former second world war bomber pilot with a fast line in chat and a fondness for the bottle. In the small town of Maysville, Kentucky, the Clooneys were a big deal.

Uncle George decided to make them bigger, taking the sisters out on the road. Betty stuck at it for three years before opting out, while Rosemary went on to score a hit record with Come On-a My House, as well as starring alongside Bing Crosby and Danny Kaye in the movie White Christmas.

Nick Clooney, meanwhile, relocated to

nearby Lexington, Kentucky, and began his broadcasting career, later becoming president of the Bluegrass Press Club. One of his tasks was to escort contestants from the local Miss Lexington beauty pageant to dinner, one of whom was a woman named Nina.

'Over dinner,' Nick recalled to Premiere, 'it was: "Pass the butter, and will you marry me?"'

She said yes and two children, Ada and George (born in 1961 and named after Nick's uncle) quickly followed.

Nick had grown up in the shadow of divorced parents, still something of a stigma in small-town America at the time. 'My parents divorced when my sisters Rosemary and Betty and I were little kids,' he told The News of the World. 'So I was determined that my kids wouldn't suffer that way.'

If anyone did suffer it was Nina, who ended up sacrificing her career for the sake of her family. 'My mother was 19 when she had my sister and 20 when she had me,' George recalled to OK magazine. 'She was in the Miss Kentucky pageant at the time and wanted to be a dancer. I think she had a more frustrating time than any of us ... she had to give up a lot. I remember her telling stories about flying to Los Angeles with a

George's father Nick Clooney & his aunt Rosemary Clooney

one- year-old and a two-year-old. It sounds like a nightmare to me – by yourself, without people helping you. That's not fun.' By the age of five, young George was already fascinated by his father's work, manning the control booth while his father read the weather after his radio news slot, and occasionally chiming in with the temperature. When Nick relocated the family to Cincinnati to host a live daily variety show, George discovered the world of television. Soon, he was helping out both behind the scenes and on air, doing everything from holding cue cards to warming up the audience (his knack with a joke was picked up from his favourite uncle, George), and even occasionally singing on air if a guest was late or failed to show.

George recounted this period of his life in detail to Sky magazine: 'My father had a live talk show when I was growing up in Cincinnati, Ohio, and I played characters on it. When it was St Patrick's Day I was a leprechaun with a cigar, and at Easter I was a rabbit with a cigar. It was live, vaudevillian television that hasn't really been around since. It wasn't like I was ever paid on my dad's show, it wasn't like we were little shitheads with cash – you did the show and then you cleaned up the set afterwards. It was a good way to grow up. When you're a kid you always have fantasies and play games and I got to act mine out with props and hats, so it was great fun.'

As a result of his own disrupted childhood, Nick insisted his family were a part of his working life.

'The important thing was that both kids were very involved in the TV shows,' he said in The News of the World. 'George was backstage at all of them. Ada passed out cups of coffee and doughnuts – she never cared for showbusiness. But George revelled in it.'

When his father asked him what he wanted

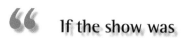

"If the show was doing well you got a **big present** for **Christmas "**

to be when he grew up, George, naturally enough, replied, 'I wanna be famous.'

However, what sounds like an idyllic childhood was sometimes anything but. In the late 1950s, Nick Clooney tried to crack Hollywood and failed, consigning himself to a life of being a big fish in a small local televisual pond. 'In the microcosm of Cincinnati, my father was Johnny Carson,' George told Vanity Fair in 1996, and while Nick was often successful, he had more than his share of ups and downs, forcing his family to relocate time and time again.

'Everything depended on the ratings,' explained George. 'If the show was doing well you got a big present for Christmas. If it wasn't, you didn't.'

However, it wasn't so much the constant motion as the changes in lifestyle that have stayed with George, whose father never allowed for the fact that his fortunes might change.

" I'm smarter about

money, or have some

sense that maybe

I won't blow

everything **"**

*Rosemary Clooney
singing on her NBC
radio series in 1953*

'It was Gulliver's Travels,' he told Vanity Fair. 'We'd live in a mansion in Kentucky, and then we'd move to a trailer, then to a nice house. It gives you a sense of how quickly your career can fall apart and how quickly you can get it back, too. It was the weirdest life in the world.'

Often, the family was forced to eat at the Beef and Boards, a regional dinner theatre where Nick, always the small-time celebrity, performed in musicals, literally singing for his – and his family's – supper.

George has never publicly displayed anything but admiration for his father and, to his credit, Nick held the family together under the most trying of circumstances. Yet it is clear that these events influenced George and did more than just inspire his interest in television. Despite his father's example, forged in the light of his own parents' divorce, George remains one of Hollywood's professional bachelors, constantly informing the press that marriage (after one brief, failed attempt) and children are definitely not on the cards for him. Occasionally, he has also let slip in interviews how much he has learnt from his

father's example: 'I'm smarter about money, or have some sense that maybe I won't blow everything,' he guardedly told Vanity Fair, shortly after signing a three-picture deal for $28m in 1996. 'I mean, let's leave a little over here so we don't end up in a trailer.'

For all the success of his parents – Nina also had her own TV talk show for a while – the spectre of failure played a large part in George's childhood. When confronted with his own transient lifestyle, he looked to the glamour of his Aunt Rosemary: 'I was really very jealous of my cousins and the life they lived in California,' he confessed to Vanity Fair. 'In my estimation they were rich. I remember seeing the tennis court and the pool and thinking, God, it's just amazing.'

However, by this time, Aunt Rosemary's star was no longer in the ascendant. She still serenaded the Kennedys, but after the assassination of Bobby she rapidly went into decline, becoming addicted to prescription drugs and spending some time in a psychiatric hospital.

From an early age, George saw the downside of fame. It is something that has kept him level-headed and often pessimistic, despite

> ## " I was terrible at
> # fighting.
> Everybody **kicked**
> my **ass** "

his own growing stardom. He constantly undercuts interviewers, explaining just how aware he is of his own sell-by date. 'Guys like Harold Lloyd and Buster Keaton owned the world at one point,' he said in the Express On Sunday, 'and then they vanished into oblivion. These guys were kings and tragedy struck. Tragedy is always going to strike.'

When George was seven, tragedy did indeed strike. His father lost his job and everyone at school knew about it: it even made the local paper. 'Clooney Gets Canned' ran the headline, and the other kids at school were quick to point it out to George and his sister. By the time Nick arrived to pick the kids up, they were inconsolable.

'So we got in the car,' Nick recalled in Vanity Fair, 'and I thought what to do. So I said, "Remember when George Gobel was here last week and you had the whole class down to the station and lorded it over them? Well, there's no free lunch. When their fathers get fired, no one knows about it. When you get to be famous and meet all those famous faces, well, here's the payback." '

It may have been a particularly harsh way to learn a lesson, but it was a lesson that young George assimilated well and truly.

The loss of Nick's job led to a period of unemployment, followed by yet another relocation. 'I was terrible at fighting,' George later said in the Daily Mirror, recalling the inevitable conflicts that would result from being the new boy in town. 'Everybody kicked my ass.'

Having trailed around big towns and trailer parks, and with George having attended five schools in eight years, Nick Clooney eventually decided that he wanted some stability in his family life, and to raise his children in a healthy, small-town environment.

'When the kids were a bit older I decided we'd move to the tiny town of Augusta in Kentucky,' Nick told the News of the World. 'It wasn't a popular idea with them, or my wife Nina. But gradually they agreed it was a wonderful place to grow up. George was hard-pressed to get away with anything because all the neighbours knew the kids and kept an eye on them. He drank too many beers at parties a few times like other boys, but he never smoked pot or even cigarettes. George had an incredible sense of humour and was the funniest kid in town. He was clearly developing his skills as an actor even in high school.'

Throughout his teenage years, George remained as closely involved as ever with his father's TV shows, acting as unofficial floor and prop manager for The Nick Clooney Show, still occasionally appearing on air in sketches and sometimes even filling in with a song.

As a child, George had lived and breathed the TV studio, once telling his father that he was 'having trouble with my audio' when he caught laryngitis. By his mid-teens, George could see it for what it was – a job, and one without guarantees – and he decided to

pursue his other love: sport. He played baseball well and, being a good hitter, he tried out for the Cincinnati Reds. Unfortunately, a good hitter was all he was, lacking a decent throwing arm.

College seemed to be the next-best option. 'To George, school was a very large restaurant and nightclub,' his mother Nina remarked in Vanity Fair in reference to her son's scholastic achievements. For at Northern Kentucky University George followed his Uncle George's example rather than his father's, opting to major in booze and partying. After three years he dropped out, taking a job cutting tobacco. 'That was how you made a living in Kentucky' he observed in Sky magazine, 'a miserable, miserable way to make a living.'

Nick harboured hopes that George would become a news anchor – while at university, he had worked briefly as a broadcaster for a news magazine show. 'I knew I would always be compared to my father,' said Clooney in The Daily Mirror. 'And I knew I could never be that good.'

It would, in fact, be another uncle (husband to Aunt Rosemary), the Oscar-winning actor José Ferrer, and his cousin, the actor Miguel Ferrer, who would show him the way forward.

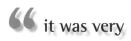

> **"** it was very
>
> # seductive,
>
> ### with beautiful
>
> # women paying
>
> ## attention to these guys **"**

George's first impression of being on a film set

Out of college and stuck in the tobacco fields, George's life was clearly lacking direction – then he received a phone call from his cousin, Miguel Ferrer. Miguel was establishing himself as an actor (he would later deliver impressive performances in Twin Peaks and the acclaimed mini-series adaptation of Stephen King's The Stand). Miguel and his father José were filming a horse-racing movie, And They're Off, in Kentucky, and they suggested that George come by and hang out. Having exposed himself to the world of television via his father's shows, George had long since lost interest in the entertainment world, but he agreed to go along and see his cousin anyway.

Once on set, however, George's performing instincts were reawakened, not least by the fact that he saw how attractive actors were to women.

'It was very seductive,' he admitted to TV Times, 'with beautiful women paying attention to these guys.'

Noticing George's good looks, the director suggested he should give acting a try, and he cast him in a small role in the movie.

'He came and camped out in my hotel room for the next three months,' Miguel told Vanity Fair. 'We played practical jokes, drank too much and had sex with a million women.'

Clooney clearly enjoyed the attention that being in front of the camera brought him. He decided that he would try and become an actor, a profession that would allow him to work in an industry he already knew and loved, while also enabling him to step out of his father's shadow. 'I fell in love with the whole industry,' he told Vanity Fair. 'I never thought I'd make any money at it, but I just loved doing it.'

George's movie debut was never released,

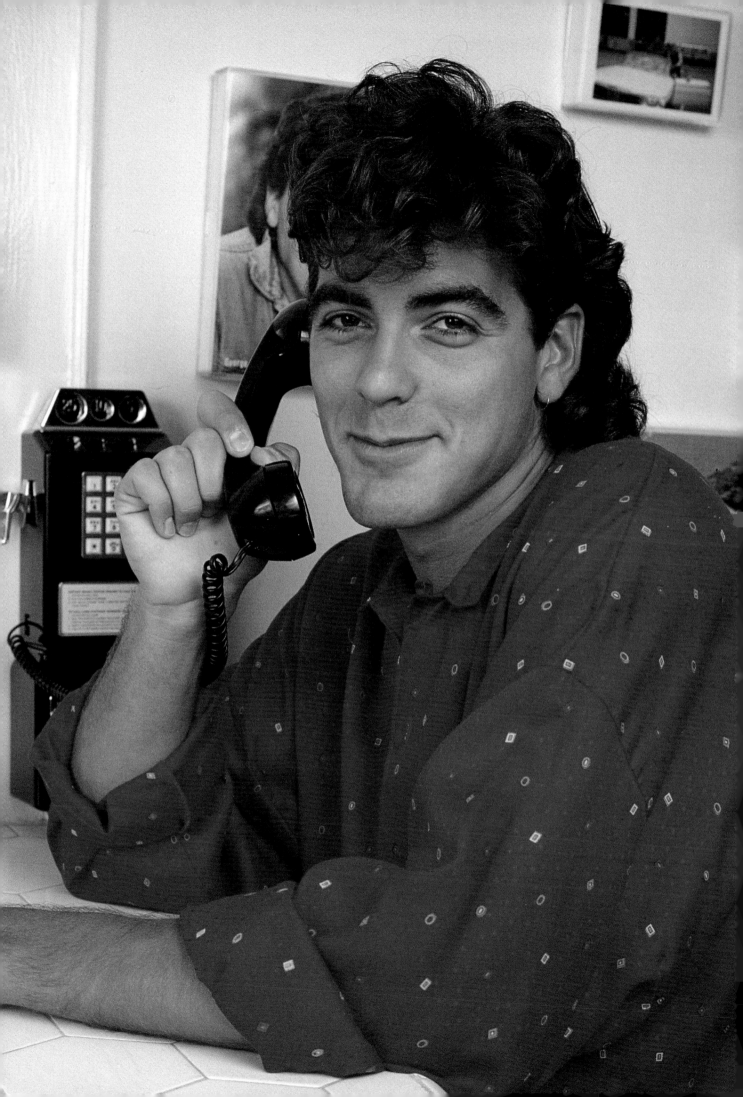

Promotional poster for Red Surf (1990)

" I've done some **terrible** films...

I didn't do it **unless** it had

a **'return'** in the title **"**

and he spent the next few months working to save money. As well as cutting tobacco, he drew caricatures in local shopping malls and sold women's shoes and insurance. With a few hundred bucks saved, and his beat-up Ford newly christened the Danger Car, George announced to his family that he was off to make it big in Hollywood as an actor. His father Nick, still obviously smarting from his own failure to crack it, was against the idea.

'When George said he was planning to go to Hollywood to be an actor, I told him he was crazy,' Nick later told the News of the World. 'The rejection you suffer is cruel and very usual. You're either too short or too tall, too this or too that. It's asking for a lifetime of rejection. But like most kids, he ignored his dad completely and did what he wanted to do.'

Nick soon accepted the idea, however, and offered his son a piece of advice that he held dear. 'He told me that you're never as bad as they say you are when they say you're bad, and you're never as good as they say you are when they say you're good,' George told Vanity Fair. 'Once you understand that, you'll survive just about everything.'

George's first stop was at his Aunt Rosemary's house, where he spent several months. While he was clearly in love with the idea of acting, Clooney was not handling the practicalities of the job very well, lacking a Screen Actors Guild (SAG) union card, and averaging about one cattle-call audition a week. In the interim, he worked as Rosemary's chauffeur, a role that quickly distanced him from the family.

'I will never really get over how humiliated I was,' he would later tell Premiere. 'Humiliated in the sense that we'd all be sitting around and they'd go: "Okay, let's all go to dinner. George, you stay here." '

No doubt taking a tip from his namesake, George was continuing to party hard. 'He

Return of the Killer Tomatoes (1988)

" That was the **bravest** thing I've **ever** seen a **vegetable** do "

Starring with Elliott Gould in the comedy series ER in 1985

" ...I noticed he had **dark** circles under his **eyes**, and he was **awful young** for that "

Rosemary Clooney on George's lifestyle

> **"** I married a **terrific** girl, a great **lady**, and it **didn't** work out **"**

With ex-wife Talia Balsam

ran pretty wild,' his Aunt Rosemary told Vanity Fair. 'I was on the road a lot, but I noticed he had dark circles under his eyes, and he was awful young for that.'

After a year, George was kicked out of his aunt's house. He ended up staying with friends, and on one occasion lived in the walk-in closet of actor Thom Matthews.

'I could never understand how he got girls in that closet with him,' Matthews told Premiere magazine. 'What could he possibly say to get them in there?'

(Clooney would return the favour in 1996, putting up the recently divorced Matthews in his Hollywood hills home.)

He drove a 1960 Oldsmobile, complete with furry dice hanging from the rear-view mirror, and did construction jobs to keep afloat. His first proper acting role in

Hollywood was in an advert for Japanese stereos. This was followed by his first real movie role, opposite Charlie Sheen and Laura Dern in Grizzly II – The Predator. Shot in 1982, this was a sequel to Grizzly, a 1976 sub-Jaws exploitation flick about a killer bear. Like his first movie, this was also never released.

'We shot Grizzly in Budapest,' Clooney told Fangoria magazine. 'It was supposed to take place in northern California, but it was cheaper to film in Hungary ... They had nothing but horrible effects. In Hungary, it's cheaper to kill a couple of Hungarians than to get fake blood ... As big stars as Charlie and Laura have become, the movie has never come out – not even on video – because it's so bad.'

However, it did set the tone for what was to

> " ...when you **first** start out as an **actor**, you read every script as if **Barry Levinson** is going to **direct** it "

follow, a string of movies that did little to advance Clooney's career. 'I've done some terrible films,' Clooney onced joked to TV Times. 'Like Return of the Red Surf, Return of the Killer Tomatoes – I didn't do it unless it had a "return" in the title.'

Return of the Killer Tomatoes (1988) – another sequel to a low-budget genre flick, in this case the 1978 killer-vegetables-on-the-rampage classic, Attack of the Killer Tomatoes – saw Clooney deliver the immortal line: 'That was the bravest thing I've ever seen a vegetable do.'

Clooney recalled the movie in 1995to Fangoria: 'That was campy as hell. It was such a horrible movie, but it was fun to do. It's one of those movies where you read the script and it's hysterically funny, and when you first start out as an actor, you read every script as if Barry Levinson is going to direct it. You think, God this is going to be great, and then, of course, it's done for £500,000, it looks like shit and it's badly directed. It still kind of works in a sad, embarrassing way.'

Return to Horror High (1987) saw him losing his head – quite literally: 'I did Return to Horror High as a favour to a friend of mine,

(director) Greg Sims,' he continued to Fangoria. 'I would fly out on weekends from Chicago, where I was doing a play at the Steppenwolf (the renowned theatre company) and shoot my scenes. It became the bane of my existence to do that movie. They didn't have enough money to do a good prosthetic head for Horror High, so they stuck my head through a trash can and put this piece on my head to look like it's been cut off.'

Greg Sims was also responsible for the action movie Red Surf (1990 – there was no 'Return' in the title), which saw Clooney cast as an ex-surfing-champion-turned-drug-dealer.

The TV movie Sunset Beat (1990) saw George taking the lead in a film that was clearly designed to ape Johnny Depp's TV show 21 Jump Street, while Combat High (1986), also made for TV, was distinguished only by the fact that the writer, George Gipe, died during production from a fatal bee sting.

Although movies were not proving to be the promised land for George, he was making a decent living and, following a unique

George with former fiancee Kelly Preston

Starring with Connie Sellecca in the Baby Talk pilot show in 1990

> **"** It's my **schlong** hanging **out** there, **not yours "**

George to producer Ed Weinberger on set of Baby Talk

audition for John Crosby, the head of casting at the ABC television network, he found himself increasingly in demand on television. Clooney was due to perform a ten minute scene from Neil Simon's play Brighton Beach Memoirs. Knowing that the scene took place on bunk beds, Clooney had a group of friends rapidly set them up before the audition. Crosby was impressed and offered Clooney a contract that night.

Ironically, his first permanent job was a recurring role in a sitcom called ER, ten years before he hit the big time on the series of the same title. Elliott Gould took the lead and Clooney played a young intern. The show was not a hit, lasting one season, but Clooney was still very much in demand with the networks. Over the next few years he landed recurring roles on five other shows, including such successful sitcoms as Facts of Life and Sisters, as well as Bodies of Evidence.

His most notable role during this period was playing the womanising factory boss of Roseanne and her sister Jackie on the number one sitcom Roseanne. While the role brought him a fair amount of attention, it was never really developed, and Clooney left after one year.

During this period, it became clear that Clooney was on his way to becoming a star – he just didn't know how to get there. Neither did the networks, who, sure of his star potential, cast him in fifteen pilots, none of which sold as a series.

None the less, all this work was making him very successful. His cousin Miguel joked to Premier that George was 'the richest guy in showbusiness that nobody knew'.

Clooney's characters have always displayed a carefree, almost flippant approach to certain aspects of their lives, and this is a trait that clearly comes from the actor himself who, while still dreaming of a successful movie career, was prepared to drift through television and a series of bad movies.

His personal life at this point was equally

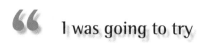

> **"** I was going to try and do the **best television** that I could **"**

unstable, with his reputation as a womaniser beginning to grow, as he was seen out and about with a string of young actresses. In 1984, while working on a play, he started dating actress Talia Balsam, the woman he would later describe as 'the one girl I truly loved'. None the less, the relationship didn't work out and Clooney threw himself into a string of liaisons, culminating in a romance with Kelly Preston.

Within twenty days of meeting, they had bought and moved into a $1million home. He gave her Max, a pot-bellied Vietnamese pig, for her birthday, and not long after, George and Kelly became engaged. In 1989, People magazine named them both as up-and-coming stars. 'The most important thing in my life is my relationship with Kelly,' George told the magazine. Shortly after, they spilt up. Kelly went on to marry John Travolta, while George assumed custody of the increasingly large Max.

Soon after, George met up with Talia Balsam once again. On impulse, they were married in Las Vegas by an Elvis impersonator.

'Afterwards, we went gambling. I'd already done the big gamble, so I figured, How much more could I loose?' he told TV Times.

Almost as soon as the vows were spoken, however, the freewheeling Clooney realised the marriage was not going to work. The couple were divorced three years later.

'I married a terrific girl, a great lady and it didn't work out,' Clooney told the Daily Mirror. 'That it didn't work out was mostly my fault. When things started to go wrong, I wasn't willing to try and fix them. I just wanted to chuck it all in, and that's not the way it should be in marriage.

'I probably – definitely – wasn't someone who should have been married at that point,' Clooney explained to Vanity Fair. 'I just don't feel like I gave Talia a fair shot. I was responsible for the failure of that marriage.'

'When I became George's wife,' Balsam told the People, 'it was as if he didn't even like me. He spent more time with his friends than with me. He didn't seem interested in our marriage.'

'Talia is a lovely girl,' Nick Clooney told the News of the World. 'George blames himself for the divorce, which is characteristically gallant of him. But he's too tough on himself. In truth, neither was to blame ... There was just too much going on in their lives to give marriage the effort it needed. They both wound up getting hurt, which is really too bad. Now George says that he's never going to get married again, that he doesn't want kids or even a serious relationship with a woman. But I know George, and some great woman is going to

George with Julia Duffy on the set of Baby Talk in 1991

The cast of *Bodies of Evidence*

"I fell in love with the whole industry. I never thought I'd make any money at it"

come along and knock him right off his feet. He will be a great husband and father – though I hope he waits until he is at a point in his career where he can devote himself to a relationship.'

The divorce was an acrimonious one, with just about every possible point being contested. Clooney calims, 'I would say to Talia, "You tell me how much, what you think is fair, I'll write the check. I won't negotiate." Instead I paid $80,000 in lawyers' fees. And that makes me crazy.'

Matters were made worse by the sudden death of Clooney's beloved Uncle George, from cancer. The 64-year-old died in his nephew's arms, and his last words were 'What a waste'.

Fuelled by this devastating event, Clooney, a man who had always lived impulsively, determined to kick his live-for-the-moment philosophy into an even higher gear.

'I'm not gonna wake up at 64 and say, "What a waste".' he told Premiere. 'Life is too short. If I walk outside and get hit by a bus, everybody'll say, "He crammed a shitload into 34 years." '

If his personal life was in tatters, augmented by a bleeding ulcer developed during the divorce, Clooney's career was reaching a

similar breaking point. He lost a pivotal movie role in Ridley Scott's Thelma & Louise to Brad Pitt. Pitt went on to become a huge movie star, while Clooney went on to appear as a transvestite in a gold bra, dancing to Belinda Carlisle's Heaven Is a Place on Earth, in The Harvest. 'It was just fun and a joke at the time,' he told the Sunday Mirror. 'I never thought anyone would ever see it.'

It was on television, however, that things came to a head. Clooney was cast in Baby Talk, a sitcom spin-off from Look Who's Talking, the film that relaunched the career of John Travolta (now married to George's ex, Kelly Preston). It was produced by sitcom veteran Ed Weinberger, whom Clooney described to Vanity Fair as 'a man who systematically destroys people and brags about it. There was a meanness to him I'd never seen before.'

Weinberger was repeatedly rude to his cast, and one day, Clooney simply decided that he'd had enough.

As he recounted to Vanity Fair, 'At some point I said, "Don't you ever talk to these people like that again." There is that moment when you go, "OK, we're two men sitting in a room. Now, do you want to fuck with me? Forget that you're the executive producer

The cast of Facts Of Life

" the **richest** guy in showbusiness that **nobody** knew "

George described by his cousin, actor Miguel Ferrer

who could fire me, because now my job's out the window. You have nothing over me now. Now I own you. Now I'm bigger than you.'"
'He called up ABC and said that I was physically threatening him because I was standing in front of him. He hadn't had anybody stand up to him in his life, you know? That was the low point.'

Weinberger recalled the incident that cost Clooney his job somewhat differently.

'I had one confrontation with him. I remember I asked him to do something in a scene, he tried it and it seemed to work, and then he refused to do it the next day. He said, in front of the mothers of the babies and some young children, "It's my schlong hanging out there, not yours." I told him it was inappropriate dialogue. But if he makes it sound as if he were some type of hero in defence of some actress, he is going to break his arm patting himself on the back.'

Whatever happened on the set of Baby Talk, as Clooney told Vanity Fair, 'that was literally the day that changed my life.' He'd spent a decade picking up the cheques, delivering the goods and generally underachieving. He was now convinced he was never going to make it in the movies.

'I decided I was going to be as good on television as I could,' he tols Sky. 'Instead of going: "I'm not a TV actor, I'm not doing television." I was going to try and do the best television that I could and hope that, sooner or later, it would turn into films.'

His salvation came in the form of a 20-year-old movie script by Michael Crichton, which had just been resurrected for TV. Like Clooney's first regular gig in Hollywood, it was called ER.

"George **Clooney**

and the Doug **Ross** character

seemed like a **complete** fit"

Back in 1974, Michael Crichton, then still working as a doctor, part-time novelist, and nascent filmmaker, having recently written and directed the hit Westworld, penned a screenplay entitled EW (for Emergency Ward). The fast paced script focused on one twenty-four hour period in the life of a big city emergency room.

'I wanted to write something that was based in reality,' Crichton explained to Janine Pourroy, author of Behind The Scenes at ER. 'Something that would have a fast pace and treat medicine in a realistic way. The screenplay was very unusual. It was very focused on the doctors, not the patients – the patients came and went. People yelled paragraphs of drug doses at each other. It was very technical, almost a quasi-documentary. But what interested me was breaking standard dramatic structure. I understood that's what the screenplay did, but I always felt it was completely watchable.'

Unfortunately for Crichton, back in 1974, he was the only one who did.

In 1989, however, Crichton received a phone call from Steven Spielberg to discuss the possibility of making a medical drama. Crichton dusted down his screenplay, now called ER and Spielberg seemed keen to make it as a theatrical movie. Until, that is, he heard about the novel Crichton was currently working on, a tale of genetic engineering and dinosaurs, entitled Jurassic Park. ER was, once again, put on the back burner and Jurassic Park went on to become the highest grossing film of all time.

Having discovered the screenplay languishing at Spielberg's Amblin company, producer Tony Thomopolous suggested adapting it into a weekly, hour long dramatic show and brought in John Wells, a former producer on the critically acclaimed China Beach TV series, to help develop the project.

With its multi characters, multi layered plotting and rapid action, the script was still

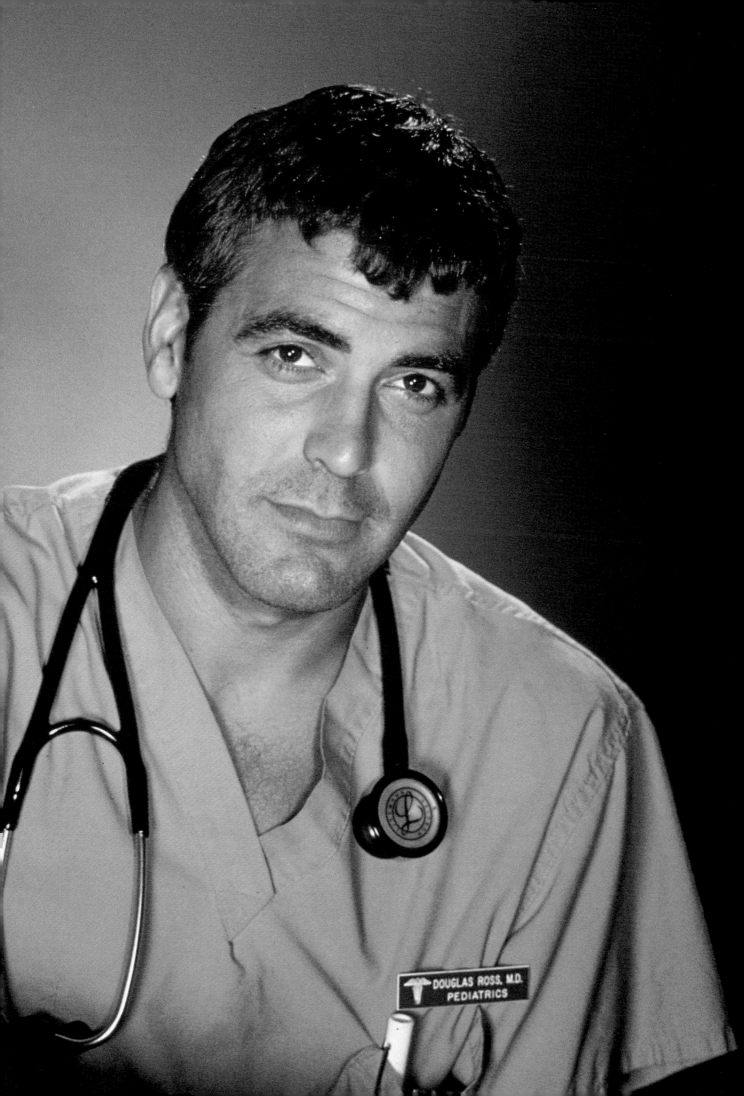

The cast of ER

   I'm just **grateful**
to be on a **show** that I'm not
embarrassed about

very unconventional for American television. Even 20 years on, as Wells explained to Pourroy, 'One of the chief complaints about the script was that you didn't know who you were supposed to care about. There wasn't a beginning, middle and end, it was really just a series of small scenes. It had multiple story lines and many stories that were just one beat and didn't go anywhere else. There was very little standard dramatic through line. But when you stepped back, they added up to an emotional tapestry that was very moving.'

Of course, there was also the fact that between them Spielberg and Crichton had just pulled off the biggest movie in Hollywood history, and nobody was going to say no to anything with their names on. In fact, Warner Bros and NBC very quickly said yes and put the two hour pilot into production.

Clooney was passed a copy of the script by a friend Jonathan Levey, involved with casting the show. Within two days of the pilot getting the go ahead, Clooney was banging down producer John Wells' door, insisting that the part of Dr Doug Ross was his.

'George Clooney and the Doug Ross character seemed like a complete fit,' Levey told Pourroy. 'If you're going to cast a character with behaviour you don't approve of – such as drinking too much and cheating on his girlfriend – you need someone who balances that behaviour with their innate charm and attractiveness. George is one of those people who can get away with pretty much anything because he's adorable.' Spurred on by Clooney's enthusiasm, and his recent popularity on the show Sisters, Wells quickly agreed, and Clooney became the first cast member of ER.

'As soon as the show got a pick up, George called me and said "Doug Ross is my part",' Wells explained. 'I hadn't even hired a

director at that point. But as soon as I hired Rod (Holcomb) – which happened to be on a Thursday – George called me again, and on Friday he came into to read for the show. He had memorised an entire scene from the pilot – the one where his character has a confrontation with the attorney who's abusing her child. He was terrific ... we hired him right away.'

With Clooney in place, Wells and his team had a reference point to base the cast around, next casting Anthony Edwards as Dr Mark Greene, as a counterpoint to George. The rest of the cast fell into place, and the pilot went into production.

On the strength of this debut outing, 24 more episodes were ordered and ER debuted in the autumn of 1994 to what was nothing short of a phenomenal reaction. Not only did it become a number one show in the States, with a 40% share of the audience, an almost unprecedented figure in this multi channel age, but it became the first hour long drama in years to assume pole position in the ratings, which had, for the past decade or more, been largely dominated by the 30 minute sitcom.

The success of the show was repeated worldwide, with critics and audiences alike becoming loyal fans.

It is a show that was always designed to be bigger than the individual actors within it, but Clooney's striking good looks and the intriguing combination of Doug Ross's heroic paediatrician contrasting with his hard drinking, womanizing lifestyle away from ER, made him the breakout star of the show. Not only did he become a major sex symbol as a result, he was also finally winning praise as an actor.

> " We both **live hard** but he's a **sad** figure and I've had a **great life** "
>
> *George Clooney on Dr Doug Ross*

"nobody comes to work in the morning **knowing** what **tachycardia** means **"**

'George was handicapped by his looks,' John Wells explained to Vanity Fair. 'There was always a sense that he was going to be a star – that's why he did so many pilots. He jumped off the screen as a great guy. But with anyone that cute and personable, it was hard to tell if he had the acting chops.'

It's easy to see why Clooney was attracted to the role of Ross. 'Doug Ross is a guy in his middle-thirties,' he told Pourroy, 'who has just discovered that all the things he used to do in life – partying a little too hard and chasing girls a little too much – are all starting to catch up to him. He is faced with having to deal with his inadequacies as an adult.'

It's a description that sounds remarkably like that of the actor himself and, while he is quick to stress the differences he does concede the similarities. 'We both live hard but he's a sad figure and I've had a great life. I do like to think I'm very professional about my job. But Doug is a little more desperate

and he's learning his way of life doesn't work.'

Much as he had drawn inspiration from his uncle George, so did the character of Doug Ross. 'I fashioned the drunk stuff after my uncle George,' he told ETV magazine. 'Al Pacino did a perfect impersonation of my uncle George in Scent of a Woman. So now I have to do a mellower version because otherwise everyone will say, "Hey, you're doing Pacino".'

The tabloid press however were quick to latch onto Clooney as new cannon fodder. His failed marriage, the impetuous and tempestuous nature of his relationship with Kelly Preston and a string of relationships with actresses, were all cited as evidence that televisions' favourite hard drinking skirt chaser was living that life off screen as well. 'I've had my share of dates, it's true,' Clooney explained to TV Times. 'But I'm not a womanizer. I've failed over the years at relationships. But they weren't total failures.

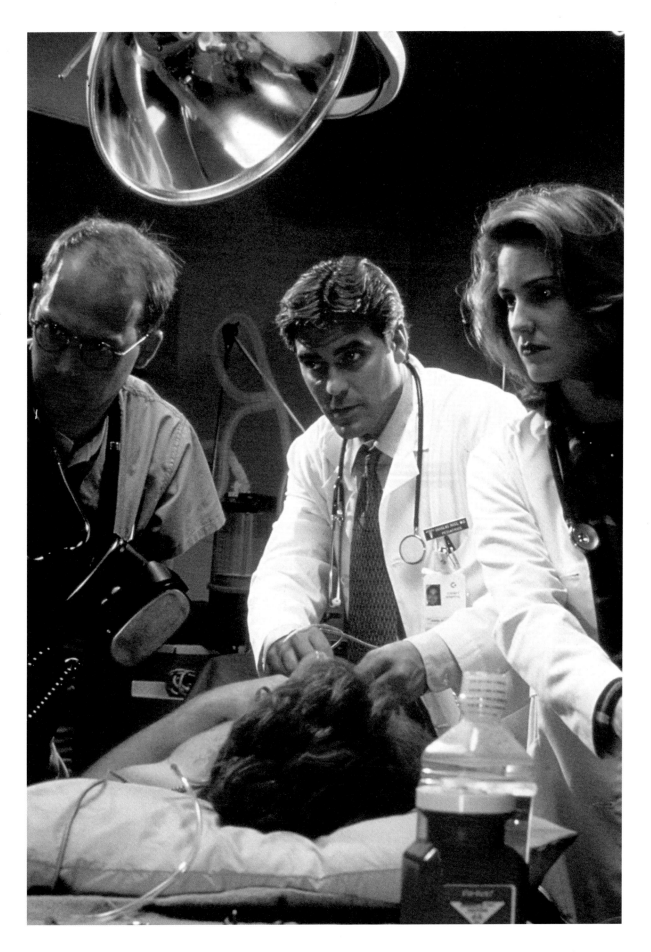

If you last together in this business for any period of time, you've kind of won.'

'People find it hard to believe but I've never formally asked a woman out,' the actor told The Sun. 'I've always gone out with people I knew. That's easier for me. I used to work as a DJ and I'd watch guys go up and hit on a girl and use those lines like, "Hey, you want to dance and see my moves?" Then I'd see these girls take those guys and pummel them and I realized I was never going to give any girl that kind of power.'

'Women are amazing and I love them. To me the most important thing in a partner is a sense of humour. People ask if I prefer blondes or brunettes. The answer is I love them all.'

Two other aspects of Clooney's private life became of strong media interest in the wake of ER. Firstly, his house. The two storey, eight bedroom Tudor house in the Hollywood hills had often acted as a refuge for George's actor friends. Now, it was painted as Hollywood's archetypal swinging bachelor pad, an image that director Joel Schumacher even contributed to, 'That house is like a sitcom,, he joked in Vanity Fair. 'He has these buddies who have recently gotten divorced, and they're all living there. There are piles of dirty laundry all over the place. I think there have been as many as three or four of them there at a time. George is like everybody's older brother. I'm 57, but if I was in real trouble, I'd go see George.'

The reality of the situation was that George was simply remaining loyal to his friends. Thom Matthews, who had once let Clooney stay in his closet, moved in to "Casa de Clooney" when he split from his wife, as did another actor friend Matt Adler. All three of their wedding rings were ceremoniously hung on display on the mantel under a dragon sculpture. 'This place is like Free

"People find it hard to believe but I've never formally asked a woman out"

GC

> **"George** is like everybody's **older brother**. I'm 57, but if I was in **real trouble**, I'd go see George **"**

Director, Joel Schumacher

Willy.' Clooney quipped in The People. 'Get him back on his feet and back to the ocean.'

Then of course, there was Max the pig, who not only had the run of the house but was on many occasions to be found sharing the bed of one of Hollywood's most eligible bachelors. Most memorably, as noted in Hollywood Confidential, on the night of the 1994 Los Angeles earthquake.

'Max was in the bed with me and woke up minutes before it happened. And I was yelling at him for waking me up – when everything just exploded. So I'm naked with Max, and running ... 'cause I'm in a house on a hill and if it's going down I want to be up on the street, dodging the next house. My buddy, who lives in the downstairs guest house, comes running up. And he's naked. With a gun because he thought someone was breaking in. And I'm trying to write a note to my folks, trying to explain to them in case we die that it's not what it seems: two naked men, a gun and a pig.'

Clooney has always displayed a penchant for elaborate practical jokes and, once again, this was something the media chose to pick upon. And why not? After all, it helped to fuel the comparisons between actor and character that were helping to make Clooney such a huge star. His highly planned pranks were further signs of an arrested adolescence, something integral to the character of Doug Ross and something that was becoming equally interwoven into the public image of the actor.

It didn't matter how much time it took, or to

" I paid my dues. When the crazy stuff started happening, I was ready – man was I ready "

what lengths he had to go, for Clooney, getting the laugh was everything, as he told Premiere magazine in 1995, recounting one such elaborate gag. Clooney was driving past a house when he saw a painting of a fat, nude, Mexican lady. Even though he described it as 'the ugliest painting you've ever seen', he rescued it from the garbage and set it aside. Over the next 16 months whenever a particular friend would ask him to play golf, George would tell him he had art classes instead. All those months later, he told his friend that he had finally produced a painting he was happy with, and gave it to him as a present. The fat, naked Mexican lady now bore Clooney signature and was still hanging in the living room of his unsuspecting pal's house when the Premiere article came out.

After nearly a decade of struggling, George Clooney had now made it as a star in Hollywood. With that came the obvious trappings of success and the actor was clearly enjoying the attention.

'I was broke, but it was a good time for me,' Clooney recalled to The Sun. 'I paid my dues. When the crazy stuff started happening, I was ready – MAN was I ready'.

ER landed Clooney a Emmy nomination for Best Actor, the attentions of Madonna, who openly flirted with him at the MTV Video Music Awards and even some highly unlikely requests from the general public – Clooney realized just what a huge impact the show was having when a total stranger asked him to be best man at his wedding.

Then, of course, there was the fan mail, as Clooney explained to ETV about one letter

" It's not me, it's **the show**. If they had a **mannequin** on ER, the mannequin would be a **star "**

he had framed in his house: 'It reads "Dear George Clooney. You are my favourite star. I love you. I love homosexual men. On your movies I'd like to see you do ... " and it goes on to specify all manner of explicit sexual acts. The note ends: "Please send me an autographed photo of you in a white shirt and tie." I love that. You can't make up stuff like that. Even in Hollywood.'

His father Nick, who with the rest of the family had relocated to LA, where he'd landed a job as presenter of the cable show American Movie Classics, was naturally enough proud of the success his son had achieved, even though he had anticipated failure for him.

'George showed incredible strength of character by never despairing and never

complaining,' he once again told the News of the World. 'Nina and I hinted he was more than welcome to come home or turn to us for help but he never did. In fact, after a few years he was taking in other struggling actors and helping them out.'

It was in an Australian airport however, that Nick realized the enormity of his son's success, when George and the rest of the cast of ER appeared on the cover of Newsweek.

'I just went bats,' he told Premiere. 'I was gauche. I was walking up to total Australian strangers, going "See this? This is my son! This is my son!"'

Despite all the attention, Clooney never lost sight of the fact that the show came first.

'It's not me, it's the show,' he insisted to ETV. 'If they had a mannequin on ER, the

mannequin would be a star. I'm just grateful to be on a show that I'm not embarrassed about.'

'I've done a lot of bad television over the years,' he elaborated to Janine Pourroy, 'and I've been very bad in a lot of bad television – so I have a pretty good perspective on what we do on ER. And I will hold what we do against any actor's job as far as difficulty goes; doing a play for eight performances a week is nothing compared to this. Every single workday is thirteen or fourteen hours long. We speak a language that we don't understand; nobody comes to work in the morning knowing what "tachycardia" means. We have to perform medical procedures as if we were professionals – and we have to do that with 50 extras flying around on a Steadicam shot with no cuts, saying: "Super ventricular tachyarrhythmia" – without screwing up. It's an ongoing all day process, and it takes great concentration.'

Not everything this long won success brought Clooney was welcome, as he quickly discovered the downside of fame. One incident on the set of the show, where he had asked an African-American extra to be quiet, resulted in a much publicized defamation charge being filed by the woman.

'She said I stood around the set in front of 30 blacks,' Clooney told Premiere, 'including the ones I work with and am very close to, and said, "let's go coon hunting some niggers." And I'm saying to myself, OK here comes the hell.'

The charge was quickly dropped.

Clooney's then current girlfriend, black actress Kimberly Russell was also quickly dropped as the pressure of working on ER and handling life in the media spotlight began to take its toll.

'It was ER that caused us to break up,' said

“ Doing a play for eight performances a week is nothing compared to this ”

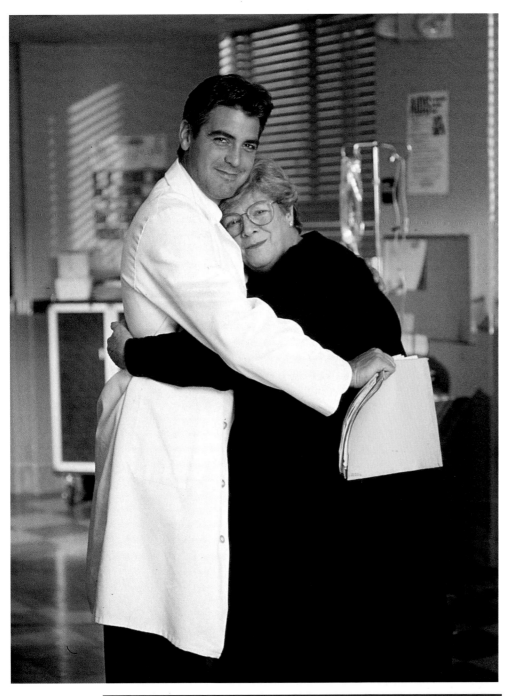

George and Rosemary Clooney on the set of ER

Russell in the Daily Mirror. 'George has become too popular for his own good. He decided he wanted to date other women'.

'The truth is I'm too busy for love,' Clooney countered in The People. 'I just don't have time for a serious relationship. My life has changed ... We work 18 hours a day on ER. If it sounds like I'm feeling sorry for myself, I'm not. I worked my whole life to get to this point and that's the danger of getting your dream, work has to come first'.

Naturally enough, rumours of rifts between the cast members soon followed hot on the heels of the show's runaway success.

'There are all these stories saying that I'm leaving the show and that Anthony Edwards and I were fighting,' Clooney told Sky Magazine. 'Tony and I are great friends, and all I've ever done is say that I won't leave the show. And then as soon as some nonsense like that comes out I get TV shows going: 'Let's go to George Clooney's home town and find out what really happened.' And one time my sister was actually dumb enough to invite them into the house!'

At the end of its first season, ER garnered a record 23 Emmy nominations, eventually winning 8 awards on the night (Clooney failed to win in the Best Actor category). Additionally, the show picked up awards from the Director's Guild, the Television Critics Association, the People's Choice Awards and Viewers for Quality Television.

'The perception has always been,' explained John Wells to Pourroy, 'that a show like this can be critically well received, but not successful. To our surprise ER has been both. During an awards ceremony, one of the network executives actually thanked me and said that because of the success of ER, he felt that it made room for other shows with the

" I just don't have time for a serious relationship "

George with Noah Wyle

 George and Julianna Margulies

"Look, this time **last year** I was reading for **three lines** in a B film"

same kind of integrity. I hope that's true.'
Throughout everything, Clooney has remained grounded, handling his fame with grace and confidence. Perhaps he just waited so long for it, that he knew what to expect when it arrived. Certainly Joel Schumacher believes this. He remarked to Vanity Fair, 'Woody Allen once said that success gives people permission to become exactly who they were always meant to be. Some people, when they get successful, punish everyone. Others, like George, are grateful. George is extraordinarily generous. It used to be called character. He has seen it all – because he is so attractive, he has been invited to all the parties. All the women stars know who he is. He has seen a lot of people self-destruct.'
Perhaps the thing that kept him the most firmly grounded are the ghosts of his childhood. Despite his new found status, Clooney was still displaying signs of being haunted by the insecurities of his father's career and own childhood. Whenever any interviewer has touched on his fame he is always quick to cite his usual references to

aunt Rosemary, or Harold Lloyd and Buster Keaton, eager to point out how ephemeral fame is and how he knows it will not last for him. 'I'm well aware that bad things will happen,' he has often stated, this time in Vanity Fair. 'If you're not, you're an idiot. Some people think I'll be able to handle the decline after the great heat. I'll go kicking and screaming but at least I'll be prepared for it, and there won't be the shock that my aunt Rosemary had ... People all of a sudden said, 'What happened to Rosemary?' Well, rock'n'roll came and women singers were out. Rosemary was on the road singing all the time. She'd been working every day. The truth is she didn't get any less talented between 1950 and 1960. In fact, she got much better. But things changed and you have to understand that.'
Things were once again about to change for Clooney. But for the better. 'Look, this time last year I was reading for three lines in a B film,' he told Premiere.
From now on it would strictly be lead roles only.

George in From Dusk Till Dawn

❝ I've been in the running for a lot of good films and I've never gotten them ❞

In 1991, in the days when George Clooney still thought the highlight of his movie career would end up being Return of the Killer Tomatoes, he auditioned for a role in a low-budget independently made heist movie titled Reservoir Dogs. The first time writer-director was a young would-be actor named Quentin Tarantino and his stylish debut movie went on to become the most influential cult movie of the 1990s.

'I must have blown them away, because I didn't get the part,' Clooney told Sky, joking over which of the colour coordinated hitmen he was hoping to play. 'Mr Magenta? Mr Fuchsia? Whatever, I didn't get the job.'

Setbacks like this and Thelma and Louise had long convinced Clooney that he was destined for the small screen.

'I've been in the running for a lot of good films,' he continued 'and I've never gotten them and, because I didn't, I thought: "Well I'm not gonna get the films now" ... I was going to try to do the best television I could and hope that sooner or later it would turn into films. In fact, I was sure that it wouldn't.'

Reservoir Dogs made Quentin Tarantino into

" I must have **blown** them away,
because I didn't get the **part** "

George on the Reservoir Dogs auditions

a player. His follow up, Pulp Fiction, set him up as the biggest new director Hollywood had seen for years, having roughly the same impact on his career that ER had had on Clooney's.

In the wake of this, Tarantino's bottom drawer was being ransacked, with just about every script he'd ever written quickly cranking up into production. Tony Scott tackled True Romance, Oliver Stone wanted Natural Born Killers. But the one Tarantino showed most interest in was his first effort, a gun toting, genre bending, guns 'n' vampires flick called From Dusk Till Dawn.

Tarantino dusted down the script, cast himself in one of the main roles and teamed up with director Robert Rodriguez to bring the movie to the screen. Rodriguez had also recently stormed Hollywood with the equally dazzling pyrotechnics of El Mariachi, made reportedly for a staggeringly

low figure of $7,000 (most of it earned by Rodriguez offering himself up as a human guinea pig to test experimental medicines). Tarantino and Rodriguez were the young turks in town and the idea of them making a movie together instantly became the hippest project in town.

The two filmmakers met at the 1992 Toronto Film Festival. Rodriguez describes their first meeting: 'Most festivals are more arts fare and here we'd made these crazy genre pictures, both our movies had these guys dressed in black, carrying guns around. So we thought, "Wow, we should make a movie together."'

From Dusk Till Dawn is, in the words of its writer, 'a head-banging, throat-slashing, blood-flowing, teeth-biting-in-the-jugular horror film.' It focuses on two brothers in crime, Seth and Richie Gecko, who, dressed in trademark ultra-cool black and on the

George bandages Quentin Tarantino's hand in From Dusk Till Dawn

"yeah, I made him a movie star"

From Dusk Till Dawn director, Robert Rodriguez

run, hijack a RV, driven by a minister who's lost his faith and his teenage children. Fate brings them to a strip bar called The Titty Twister on the Mexican border. It is here that what has so far been a taut suspense thriller takes a decidedly unusual turn – everyone in The Titty Twister turns out to be a vampire and the movie becomes a delirious celebration of on-the-screen, in-your-face, tongue-in-cheek carnage.

Tarantino wanted to play Richie and had planned to have an older character actor like Robert Blake play his brother. Rodriguez had other ideas. He had seen George Clooney on a late night satire show called Politically Incorrect. He wasn't really aware of ER; he thought he'd just seen a movie star.

'I wanted somebody younger but I didn't care for a lot of the younger actors playing that part, having to prove the whole time they were tough,' he said. 'I couldn't think of any good young tough actors that we have. And I wanted somebody that was on the rise, who was relatively fresh. And I waited around until I'd cast everybody else, then I saw George on television, doing some interviews and stuff, brooding, and I thought, wow this could be a great turn of events for him. He's playing the nice guy on TV, if he plays something completely different in this movie, he could get a younger, movie audience. Nobody was offering him movie roles at the time. His vacation was coming up and he was gonna take the time off. So yeah, I made him a movie star.'

The move from television to movie star is not always a guaranteed one. For every

Robin Williams there is a Ted Danson, for every Bruce Willis, a Tom Selleck heads back to the tube. The conventional Hollywood wisdom is, "why pay to see someone you can see at home for free?" So, despite, Clooney's enormous success of the previous year, casting him in a movie was still considered a risk by Hollywood. Similarly, for Clooney to try and make that leap in a (relatively) low budget genre-defying horror flick was not necessarily the wisest move. What the movie had in its favour was the cache of its makers.

Quentin Tarantino became convinced Clooney was right for the role when he directed the penultimate episode of the first season of ER.

'Miramax had an Oscar party, and I met Robert there,' Clooney recalled to Sky magazine. 'I was working all day and didn't make it to the actual Oscars, probably with good reason because I'm a television actor, but I met some people from Miramax and they invited me to the party. I got there and I met (producers and heads of Miramax) Harvey and Bob Weinstein and they introduced me to Robert. We got along pretty well and then Quentin was going to come in and direct an episode of ER a couple of weeks later, so I got to meet him properly as well.'

To prepare for their roles as brothers, Tarantino insisted he and Clooney spent the early part of the summer hanging out together.

Principal photography began a few weeks later in the late summer of 1995, during Clooney's summer break from ER, and the actor clearly had a blast, joking with Fangoria magazine how proud he was of the spider's web tattoo that covered his neck and ran up his face. 'Every day people come up to me and ask, "What the hell did you do?" I actually get yelled at. It's nuts. But it's even

" It's a **relief** just to

stick a gun in some **guy's**

mouth and blow

the back of his **head** off "

Harvey Keitel and George - From Dusk Till Dawn

> ❝ why **pay** to see **someone** you can see at home for **free?** ❞

Conventional Hollywood wisdom

more fun to not explain it or simply say, "I've always had this – I just cover it up with makeup".

On set with Cinefantastique magazine he discussed the similarities of his two major roles. "They're about the same except I get to wear a tattoo in this one. But the pace here is easier. On ER we're shooting nine pages a day. Our problem is not acting so much as just trying to get the words out of our mouths in a take. If you screw up, you have to start all over again, with all the extras and eight actors all working at the same time. And it's all about medical stuff and it's easy to screw that stuff up. It's a relief just to stick a gun in some guy's mouth and blow the back of his head off."

Clooney also joked about his sex symbol status, 'The actresses are now saying 'George, can we rehearse the love scene one more time?' The difficulty is you actually have to live up to that image when it comes down to it and drop your pants. But I have a stunt double now, a weenie wrangler.'

'Robert is always asking me, "George, how would you shoot this?"' Clooney continued. 'And I'd just say, "If there is some way you can just cut to me, I think you've got a movie." I'm like the dog in El Mariachi. When (Robert) did El Mariachi he didn't have a sound sync camera so later after filming he would have the actors repeat their lines into a tape recorder. He also did shots of this dog. And then every time the voices

" We had **coffee** together and I realized George was **the guy** – charming, **funny** and a little bit of a **dickhead** at the same time "

Michelle Pfeiffer

and film would get out of synch, he'd just cut to the dog. In this film, I've become that dog in a lot of the scenes.'

On set, Clooney continued to talk of the movie, while still finding time, on a more serious note, to air his constant fear of failure. 'Right now is the year of my life,' he said. 'I'm getting a lot of offers. Any film that I want next year, at any studio – they'll hold the film until I'm ready to do it. The world changed for me. And that's a great thing. But next year you can be sure it'll be me asking, "Do you want fries with that?"'

'This is much more than I could have hoped for,' Clooney told Fangoria magazine. 'I was offered a big movie at Universal but I didn't want to do that Richard Grieco (a recent TV-into-movies casualty) splash thing where you come out making $1 million on your first big movie and it ends up being cheesy ... When you're in that situation you're immediately held responsible if the film fails or not, and I don't want that responsibility just yet.'

Clooney was clearly relishing his first shot at proper movie stardom and appreciated the fact he was in good company.

'Having done some bad television and

George and Michelle getting aquainted on One Fine Day

" I'm the **luckiest** man alive ... but **watch**, it will change "

having been bad in a lot of it too,' he told Fangoria, reiterating his constant self deprecating attitude to the early stages of his career, 'I now get to work on what is arguably one of the best series of the decade with some of the best people on television. And now I'm working with the best people in films. Quentin has just won the Best Screenplay Oscar and Robert is one of the most interesting, lively and smart directors I've ever seen, let alone worked with. Then there's Harvey Keitel, whom I've been a fan of forever, and Miramax is the hottest company in the business – all of a sudden I'm in this game. I'm the luckiest man alive ... but watch, it will change'

Clooney reportedly hit it off with Keitel on set, often winding his co-star up with quips like, 'That was terrific, Harvey. Reminds me of my early work,' and offering to find him an agent next time he came out to LA.

On a more serious note, he explained to Fangoria the tight scheduling involved in juggling the movie and the impending second season of ER.

'I was Robert's first and only choice for this role and that's pretty flattering. I never thought I would get to do the movie because of the very short hiatus from the show. And there wasn't the leverage that if I did this movie, it would help the show be more successful; we had a 40 share on the series. But John Wells, the show's executive producer, is a real nice guy and said, "Let's work it out." So I'm only working one day for the first couple of episodes on the new season.'

For the latter part of the From Dusk Till Dawn shoot, this meant Clooney was working round the clock, seven days a week, which inevitably resulted in some confusion. 'I had to learn my lines while making the two hour round trip between sets,' he explained to ETV. 'Luckily, driving my Ford

Go

"The **actresses** are now saying 'George, can we rehearse the **love scene** one more time?"

Bronco is therapy for me. I worked seven days a week for forty days, finishing at three in the morning sometimes for Dusk and making it to a 6am call for ER. But I figured if I'm gonna get a shot, it won't come twice. 'There was one incident – I guess you can take the man out of ER, but you can't take ER out of the man. In one scene Quentin Tarantino has this really bloody hand and I started looking concerned. All of a sudden the director Robert Rodriguez began yelling, "You're getting into doctor mode. Cut it out." Then I remembered, "Oh yeah, I'm a killer today."'

From Dusk Till Dawn wrapped and Clooney went back to his day job on ER. As the second season progressed, the profile of Doug Ross remained prominent, culminating in one episode where Ross struggles heroically to save a young child from drowning in a flooding storm drain. The episode, designed in many way to parallel the first season's Love's Labor Lost which had highlighted Anthony Edwards, showcased Clooney as an actor at his finest, showing the strength of character and passion beneath Ross's often facile facade. It also helped earn Clooney a nomination from the Screen Actors Guild Awards.

Adding to Clooney's career trajectory even further was a tape Robert Rodriguez had assembled. 'While he was editing the film,' Clooney explained to ETV, 'he put together a trailer showcasing me, complete with fake reviews. Then he sent them round to some agents and got the buzz going. Robert said, "All we need to do is send bootleg footage around town, so people will want to see the film, and we'll get everyone stirred up about you. You'll be a millionaire before the film

" He has a roguish charm coupled with a really remarkable comic ability "

One Fine Day director, Michael Hoffman

even comes out." Well, it kind of worked. Studios who wouldn't throw me a bone with a small role before were now calling with big offers.'

From Dusk Till Dawn opened Christmas of 1995 at the top of the US box office. The critics may have been uncertain what to make of this tongue-in-cheek, blood-gushing assault, but one thing was clear, George Clooney carried himself on the big screen like a bona fide movie star.

The film's excessive approach to gore did provoke some negative criticism in terms on the on-going debate over movie violence, but Clooney had been quick to dismiss this to Cinefantastique, back on the set.

'The violence in this movie is done like Scarface. It's done seriously, but it's done so much to excess that you (realize) "they're kidding", which is fun. But, you can bet they'll be the Bob Doles who will come out on this one.'

'If you're doing a movie about two people having sex, you're glorifying sex and there isn't much of a way not to glorify anything you do,' he elaborated to Sky.

'You can take a stand and as you go up the ladder you can have more control, but I think it's very difficult because I am an employee still. So you take the jobs until you can get to the position where you say, "Stop. I'm sick and tired of seeing actors' opinions on things" ... Every time I see someone like Alec Baldwin – whom I like – or a similar showbiz star talking about politics, I think: "You're not famous for doing that so you shouldn't really take that advantage." Usually they're just idiots.'

While Clooney was busy establishing his movie career, the tabloid press were

George and Mae Whitman in One Fine Day

once again establishing his image as a hard-partying womanizer, citing relationships with a string of actresses and models, from MTV presenter Karen Duffy to model Vendela to actresses Denise Crosby, Julianne Phillips and both Lisa Kudrow and Courteney Cox of the hit show Friends, whom Clooney had met when they shot a joint ER/Friends cover for Vanity Fair's prestigious yearly television issue. (Clooney and Noah Wyle later cameoed in an episode of Friends as their characters from ER).

Clooney was clearly beginning to tire of this attention, most notably of the way he was hounded by the new style "videorazzi", camcorder carrying "reporters" who stalked and taped celebrities in order to sell the footage to an increasing amount of cheaply produced "reality television" news shows.

'I was involved in a real awful semi-scandal,' he confessed to Sky magazine in reference to the extra who had accused him of racism on the set of ER the year before. 'The defence is it never happened, but they sell it to this tabloid show Current Affair and they're trying to run the story, and then a pressure group leaks the story to the LA Times who run it.

'Eventually, of course, they print a retraction because it didn't happen. But I am now burned because of that and the reason I'm burned is because I'm on a very popular show and the names ER and George Clooney will make someone say: "Hey, what is that?" and pay for a magazine to see what happened. Damn all of the facts, damn everything, the important thing is to sell it,

> " He's definitely **trouble** ..., been **there**, done **that** "
>
> *Michelle Pfeiffer*

" from **my experience** of **working** with him, he is about as **nice** as they come "

Michelle Pfeiffer

and that's frustrating for someone who is a liberal and believes in journalism and the freedom of the press.'

Luckily, for Clooney, such incidents were simple distractions, given how his movie career was kicking into high gear. At one point he was receiving around one offer a day from the major studios, eventually signing to play the lead in a big budget update of The Green Hornet. A radio serial from the 1930s, The Green Hornet had been turned into a successful 1960s show by the team responsible for the TV version of Batman. It was hoped that a Green Hornet movie would create an instantly successful franchise.

However, before donning the mask of The Green Hornet, Clooney once again pulled a double shift, filming ER and a new movie, One Fine Day, simultaneously.

In this old fashioned romantic comedy,

Clooney played carefree newspaper columnist Jack Taylor, who, when forced into looking after his five-year-old daughter for the day, meets and falls in love with uptight architect Melanie Parker (played by Michelle Pfeiffer) who's also looking after her son (Alex Linz).

'Because of our different schedules,' Clooney said on set, 'Michelle would shoot one of her scenes first and I'd film mine later, listening to playback in my ear. It came down to timing – memorising exactly when she pauses and when they would be speaking. I began to get the hang of it ... after about the thirtieth take.'

The original idea for the movie stemmed from its producer Lynda Obst's personal life, 'I was having a spectacularly impossible day, logistically, in which I was trying to do my job and deal with the exigencies of a teenage son. My situation, it turned out, was quite

similar to that of several of my friends who had their own share of hellacious career/child juggling days. I suddenly realized that the new definition of heroism was simply surviving the day as a working mother.'

One Fine Day showcased a side of Clooney that hadn't had much of an airing before. Its success at the box office, once again showed Hollywood that here was a force to be reckoned with – a leading man who could not only do action and dispatch vampires but also deliver quick witted comic repartee, creating a strong on screen chemistry with one of Hollywood's top actresses.

'He has a roguish charm coupled with a really remarkable comic ability' explained the director Michael Hoffman to Vanity Fair. 'He's like watching Cary Grant. Men will like him because he's a respectable and viable advocate for their position. And women obviously love him.'

Clooney admitted to Film Review, that he had some trouble adjusting to the autonomy of the movie director after his experiences on TV, 'In television it's not easy to be directed because you have a different director every week. Each tries to make this the ER episode that Dr Ross cries. If you're doing one episode that would be fine, but you're not, you're doing twenty two. You're the landlord of this character, so you have to watch out for it. It was very difficult for me to work on a feature film and to do what Michael Hoffman asked. He would say, "Do this" and I wouldn't do it. And he would come over and say, 'You're not doing it'. And he was right. I had to change my ways a little bit, and thank God because he was right on every instinct that he had. He's got great comedic instincts. He's an amazing director'.

'We had coffee together,' co-star Michelle Pfeiffer told TV Times, 'and I realized George

" Everything

I am doing now is **geared** towards

finding **better** and better

material and doing **serious** work "

The Movies —

> **"Men** will like him because he's a **respectable** and viable **advocate** for their position. And **women** obviously love him **"**
>
> *Director Michael Hoffman*

was the guy – charming, funny and a little bit of a dickhead at the same time.'

'He's definitely trouble – bad, been there, done that,' Pfeiffer joked to Vanity Fair. 'He was certainly not as narcissistic and self-centred as some I've worked with. He doesn't take himself that seriously. I had to be the responsible one. But, for all the bravado, there's something very vulnerable about him.'

Clooney had worked with Pfeiffer's sister DeeDee on Sunset Beat and the two had briefly dated. 'She still speaks highly of him,' Pfeiffer confessed 'and from my experience of working with him, he is about as nice as they come'.

'I have known Michelle on and off for 13 or 14 years,' Clooney explained to Film Review. 'I dated her sister, Dee Dee, we did a movie together and we're very good friends. I've met Michelle at certain times but I really didn't know her well.'

'Everything I am doing now is geared towards finding better and better material and doing serious work,' he continued to The Express. 'Working with Michelle Pfeiffer was an unbelievable experience. One Fine Day is a film that will remind people of the kind of movies that were made in the 30s and 40s, when there was still some romance in the world. When I finished that movie, I told myself that this is what I've been fighting for. I've wanted my shot and now I'm taking it. I struggled for ten years and then got a break, and it's funny when you think of the career I've had and the number of bad TV shows and movies such as Return of the Killer Tomatoes – and that was the best film I did. So the most important thing is to enjoy the ride'.

Helping him enjoy it further was a call he received from one of his executive producers.

Steven Spielberg, along with former Disney

" ...the most **important** thing is to enjoy the **ride** "

head honcho Jeffrey Katzenberg and record and film producer David Geffen had recently established their own autonomous studio, DreamWorks SKG. Their first project was to be a post-Cold War thriller titled The Peacemaker.

'Steven (Spielberg) sent me a note that said, "This is our first project at Dreamworks and you're my first choice to do it", Clooney told ETV. 'He got me out of my commitment to The Green Hornet so I'd be free to do it.'

The Peacemaker was shot on location in Europe over the summer break from ER, with Emmy-winning ER director Mimi Leder calling the shots. A suspense thriller, based on real events, The Peacemaker focused on the hunt to trace a train load of Russian ICBMs, due to be dismantled following the end of the Cold War, but now mysteriously missing in Southern Russia. Clooney played Col Thomas Devoe, a member of the US Army's elite Special Forces, teamed with nuclear physicist Dr Julia Kelly (Nicole Kidman), in a race against time to uncover the terrorist behind a potential worldwide nuclear disaster.

During filming, in reference to Clooney's constant insistence in the press that he would never marry again or have children, Nicole Kidman bet him $10,000 that he would be a father before he turned 40.

Michelle Pfeiffer matched that bet. 'He has a real love-hate relationship with kids,' she told Vanity Fair, 'but once he gets started, he'll have 10.'

'Kids are a huge responsibility and I don't think I'm the most responsible person in the world,' retorted Clooney in the Express. 'No way am I going to lose my money on this one. The deal is for twenty grand. I can get a vasectomy for $5,000 and I'm $15,000 up. Right there I can make a profit.'

Clooney need not have worried about the money. His next deal would see him take on the mantle of one of the most financially successful franchises in Hollywood history, picking up a pay cheque somewhere in the region of $28 million into the bargain.

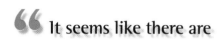

❝ It seems like there are

no limits on what these shows

can put on air about your **private life ❞**

George on his run-in with Hard Copy producer, Frank Kelly

Having spoken out against the media several times in interview, Clooney decided to take things to the next level in 1996. Entertainment Tonight was America's leading media magazine show, a show on which Clooney had been interviewed numerous times. Its producers were also responsible for a show called Hard Copy, a "news" show that relied heavily on amateur video footage. Hard Copy was a prime example of the increasing trend of "reality television", itself a direct result of the availability of camcorders. Any footage with a celebrity, no mater how it was attained, was deemed newsworthy.

Given his star status and his reputation, Clooney was a perfect target for the show, and had featured so often that he realized something had to be done. He talked to the producer, Frank Kelly and struck a deal – he would do Entertainment Tonight (ET) if he wasn't featured on Hard Copy. For a while it worked, but then Kelly reneged on the deal, causing Clooney to send the producer of ET a memo that soon became public knowledge, here's how it appeared in Empire:

'To The Producers of 'Entertainment Tonight: Well, we gave it a shot. And for a six month period Frank Kelly kept his word. My name wasn't on Hard Copy and I did several interviews for you. I guess the statute of limitations for keeping your word is about six months for Mr Kelly, or maybe it was a landmark, and I should feel honoured.

Last month, Hard Copy did an undercover story about my girlfriend and me. A probing in-depth report that will have great significance in the world. The story doesn't matter. The point is that he broke our deal. A deal that he proposed.

What is most amazing to me is that he offered this deal in the first place. In a letter! He actually wrote it down ... A so-called news format show will agree that they will not be covering me in any future stories, if I do his other show.

Now that's amazing!

If you're going to call a show Hard Copy implying some sort of journalistic and ethical investigating, you can't make deals to certain people not to put them on your show ... or at least you can't write it down. What an idiot!

So now we begin. Officially. No interviews from this date on. Nothing from ER, nothing from One Fine Day, nothing from Batman and Robin and nothing from DreamWorks' first film The Peacemaker. These interviews will be reserved for all press but you. Access Hollywood, E, whoever. It won't affect you much. Maybe other actors will join me. Maybe not. This doesn't matter, it's about doing what's right.

Again, I am sorry. You're a nice bunch of people and you've always treated me fairly. But your company and Mr Kelly have to be responsible for what they say.

And so do I.'

'This thing has got to stop,' he continued. 'It seems like there are no limits on what these shows can put on air about your private life. I refuse to be stalked by video cameras every time I walk on the street ... Sometimes they shout abuse, hoping to capture an angry reaction on tape. When they sneak round your parents' house and pull shit like that, a line has to be drawn.'

The main reason for George's reaction, however, was French. While filming The Peacemaker, Clooney frequented the Barfly cafe, where he met a young waitress named Céline Balitran. Entranced by the young law student, he returned to the cafe every day, eventually asking her out.

'We went for a walk and suddenly he seized me in his arms and kissed me,' Céline told Paris Match. 'I realized he was the man of my life. We realized we couldn't live without each other.'

Indeed they couldn't, with Céline rapidly

" I just **show up** and they stick me in a **suit** and I say OK **who** am I today? "

George in One Fine Day

"...fun is how I like to **work,** because I'm not all that **deep** an actor **"**

packing her bags and heading for the States and Casa de Clooney.

'Within a day I packed up and left,' she continued. 'I gave my furniture to my best friend, paid off my bills, put my papers in order and told everyone I was going to live in the US ... We are madly in love and for me a love story means marriage and babies, which may not be the wisest thing to say to a man who once vowed, "I'll never marry again and I'll never have kids."'

Marriage and kids were still out of the picture for Clooney; indeed, seeing his new girlfriend was enough of a problem. The reason being, he was still working 100 hour weeks, due to another movie offer, this one involving a certain Caped Crusader.

Tim Burton had established Batman as one of the most financially successful movie franchises in Hollywood history, blending his own darkly skewered visions with the recent growth of the 'graphic novel', a more adult approach to comics, both visually and in terms of material. After two movies, Burton left; his star Michael Keaton followed.

Warner Bros, the producer of ER, recruited reliable Joel Schumacher behind the lens and charismatic Val Kilmer in front. The result was the highest grossing film of 1995 and one of the most public director vs star feuds of recent years, with Schumacher making no bones about the attitude of Kilmer. 'I was told right from the start that Val was difficult, and he wasn't for me on Batman Forever until one day when he was

" What does **Batman** have to be **depressed** about **"**

going ballistic, and I went in and told him to shape up ... I'm really tired of overpaid, overprivileged actors,' he told Cinescape magazine. 'I don't know why we're protecting these people. Is it because we're so afraid they won't work with us again? I pray some of them don't work with me again'.

When the fourth Batman instalment fell due, Schumacher agreed to once again helm the picture; Kilmer however, chose to make The Saint, a movie that just about every major star in Hollywood had turned down. Warners needed a new face to fit the Bat-cowl. They screen tested, amongst other, David Duchovny, star of the hugely successful X Files TV series who told Film Review he 'looked great in the suit but my nose was too big'.

George Clooney's nose however, looked just right and he landed the coveted role of Batman for a reported $10 million, part of a three picture deal with Warners worth in the region of $28 million.

When he heard the part was his, the first person Clooney told was his cousin Miguel Ferrer, a life long fan of the Caped Crusader. 'I called him because his hero growing up was Batman,' Clooney explained to Cinescape. 'We used to sit around making plaster Batmans and goofy stuff like that as kids. I said to him 'Guess what I'm going to do in September? I'm going to be in Batman.' Miguel is like 'Oh that's nice. What are you going to do, be a helper or something?' I said, 'No listen – I'm going to be Batman.'"

Miguel's reaction was apparently 'unprintable because it contains so many expletives'.

Titled Batman and Robin, the fourth adventure featured Bruce Wayne's alter ego and his youthful ward Dick Grayson, taking on the might of Arnold Schwarzenegger's Mr Freeze and Uma Thurman's Poison Ivy.

George with Tom Cruise at the UK Premiere of Mission Impossible

Clueless star Alicia Silverstone, the first 18 year old in Hollywood history to ink a $10 million deal, added to the ranks of the heroes as Batgirl.

'Playing Batman is one thing – it's really fun,' Clooney told Cinescape. 'And fun is how I like to work, because I'm not all that deep an actor.'

Keeping in character, Clooney's approach was to liven up the character of Batman, eschewing the former incarnations of Michael Keaton and Val Kilmer, who both played the dual roles of Bruce Wayne and Batman as a haunted schizophrenic. 'We tried to get rid of some of the moodiness that Batman had in the other movies. I think we've seen enough of the Bat-brooding. I mean, let's think about it for a minute. Batman does not have such a tough life. The guy is loaded. He gets all the best girls. He has a cool car. What does Batman have to be depressed about?'

Once again, Clooney had managed to find a character whose basic description mirrored his own.

On set, he was even more flippant when Radio 1 cought up with him.

'I try to throw a little Dr Ross into everything I do,' he said, before going on to discuss the pressure of stepping into cinema's most public cape. 'Actually it's a lot less pressure being the third guy to play Batman rather than the second. Val had a tougher time because Michael had done two, so we've established that Batman's replaceable. My only hope is I don't screw it up. The only advantage I have is that Arnold (Schwarzenegger) is really scared of me in real life. We have a history, back when he was doing Conan ... I stunt doubled for him.' Clooney went on to explain his role in the movie, as always, adopting his self deprecating stance. 'I don't have a whole lot of acting range anyway so there isn't a

" I try to throw a little Dr Ross into everything I do "

" Arnold **Schwarzenegger** is really **scared** of me in real life. "

whole lot of difference between the things I do. I wish I could say I have a little "method" to it but I just show up and they stick me in a suit and I say OK who am I today? As long as I don't have a stethoscope around the Bat-suit, I'm fine.

'The truth is,' he confessed, touching on the more sensible, 'it's fairly easy to do. This is a profession and if you're a professional, this is fairly easy to do.'

Director Joel Schumacher, clearly still smarting from having worked with Kilmer, told Radio 1, 'The reason we're ahead of schedule is that everybody's very committed, very professional and extraordinarily talented. And I'm able to use my energies to make the movie instead of doing the jobs for the actors their parents neglected to do, like discipline them, sober them up, slap them into shape', Schumacher had nothing but

praise for his new Batman.

'Despite being a great actor and being mighty damn handsome in that black rubber, he has brought a humanity to the piece that is very important to this story ... And he's also the only Batman who can dress his own wounds', Schumacher joked..

In breaking with tradition, Clooney also talked about he 1960s Batman TV show, a camp delight that up until now has seemed light years away from the cinematic interpretation of the Dark Knight.

'When I was a kid, that TV show was a big hit ... So I grew up putting the little cape on ... I stopped about a couple of weeks ago. In the TV show I always loved Frank Gorshin as The Riddler, I thought he was a genius. But the character I liked the most is Robin.' Clooney's on set attitude was always flippant, obviously relishing his new found

George and Arnie

> **"** He likes telling people he fit into **Val's suit**, but the **codpiece** had to be made much **bigger** **"**

George and Céline Balitran

status as Hollywood's biggest superhero. He also continued to indulge his other love, basketball, ironically thrashing Superman star Dean Cain in one game on the Warners lot. Clooney's passion for the game almost halted production on Batman and Robin, when a between-scenes game on ER caused Clooney to fall badly.

Another potentially fatal incident occurred on a charter flight with the main cast.

'We had just taken off when the engine stopped and we started dropping,' Chris O'Donnell, who plays Robin, explained to Playboy. 'The stewardess was yelling, "Oh my God." That did it. My heart stopped. We were heading for another plane that was in the wrong zone. When it was over we were saying, "Bloody Marys please."'

The Batman and Robin shoot went remarkably smoothly with Clooney's only complaint being the Bat-suit itself. 'Have you ever walked around in rubber from head to toe all day long?' he asked Cinescape. 'I think they could call (it) the Batman diet. That's how hot the suit is. Buckets of sweat are pouring out of you. You feel light headed. You can't hear a thing. Plus, with that suit, it's not such a great idea to consume massive quantities of liquid, if you know what I mean. Michelle Pfeiffer, who played Catwoman, and I just worked together in One Fine Day, and it dawned on me that I should ask her for some tips. She told me to insist on a trap door in the suit, and I thought she was kidding. She wasn't kidding'.

Director Schumacher also touched on the suit while talking to Cinescape: 'George did want a new suit. He likes telling people he fit into Val's suit, but the

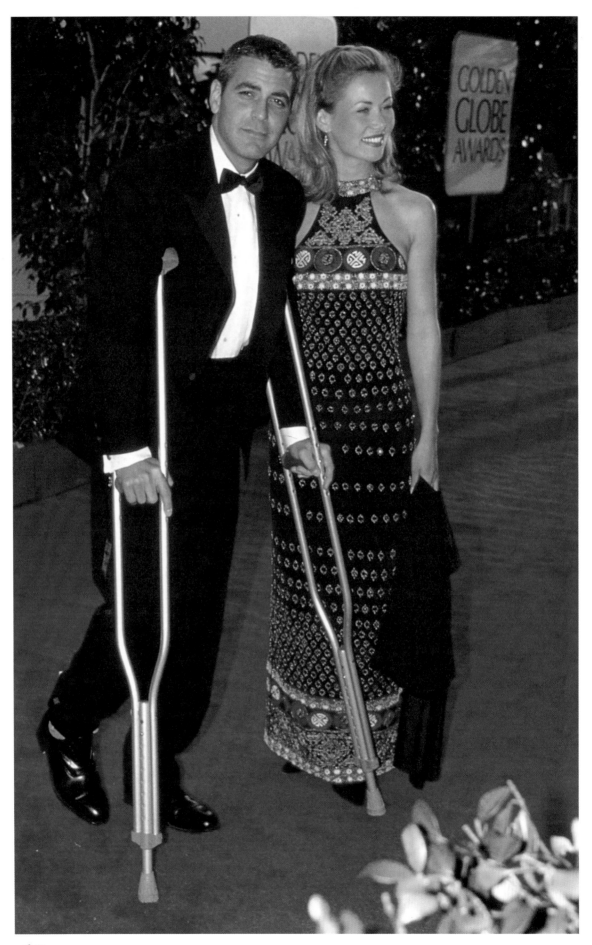

codpiece had to be made much bigger.'

Although he may still have about doubts about the longevity of his success, it's clear that the days of acting opposite deadly vegetables are long gone for George Clooney.

The third season of ER saw his salary hiked up to $100,00 per episode, making him the highest paid actor on the show. Batman and Robin confirmed his status as a movie star. Even his personal life seems to be in order. In short, George Clooney has made it. But still, the spectre of failure is ever present for the actor.

'The truth of the matter is that I'm afraid that out of laziness I could end up letting a moment pass me by that could actually put me in a position where I can choose,' he confessed in Vanity Fair. 'Because that's all I'm trying to do – get to work with better and better people. I had friends who were very successful – old men who had Academy Awards like my uncle Jose. There were things that were important to them like getting up and saying 'I'd like to thank ... ' or the movie opening. But those are just tiny little moments in your life. You look forward to them for months, and then it comes and then it's gone. So what I've learned is that you have to love the entire process. You have to love auditioning, you have to love going to work, because otherwise it all rushes by.

'I'm at the top of the roller coaster,' he concludes 'and I can't get off'.

GEORGE CLOONEY: FILMOGRAPHY

And They're Off! *(1982)*
Grizzly II - The Predator *(1986)*
Combat High *(TV - 1986 UK: Combat Academy)*
Return to Horror High *(1987)*
Return of the Killer Tomatoes *(1988)*
Sunset Beat *(TV - 1990)*
Red Surf *(1990)*
The Harvest *(1992)*
Unbecoming Age *(1992)*
Without Warning: Terror in the Towers *(TV - 1993)*
ER *(1994 - Pilot)*
From Dusk Till Dawn *(1995)*
One Fine Day *(1997)*
Batman and Robin *(1997)*
The Peacemaker *(1997)*

SOURCES CHAPTER 1	CHAPTER 2	CHAPTER 3	CHAPTER 4	CHAPTER 5
Behind The Scenes At ER	Behind The Scenes At ER	Behind The Scenes At ER	Cinefantastique magazine	Cinescape magazine
by Janine Pourroy	by Janine Pourroy	by Janine Pourroy	ETV magazine	Film Review magazine
The Daily Mirror	The Daily Mirror	The Daily Mirror	The Express	Paris Match
ETV magazine	ETV magazine	ETV magazine	Fangoria magazine	Playboy magazine
Elaine Lipworth	Fangoria magazine	Hollywood Confidential	Film Review magazine	Radio 1
Express On Sunday	The News of the World	(Plume/Penguin)	Sky magazine	Vanity Fair magazine
The News of the World	The People	Elaine Lipworth	TV Times magazine	
OK magazine	Premiere magazine	The News of the World	Vanity Fair magazine	
The People	Sky magazine	The People	Production notes from	
Premiere magazine	The Sun	Premiere magazine	One Fine Day	
Sky magazine	The Sunday Mirror	Sky magazine		
The Sun	TV Times magazine	The Sun		
TV Times magazine	Vanity Fair magazine	TV Times magazine		
Vanity Fair magazine		Vanity Fair magazine		

George Clooney